# Bumblebees Can't Fly

## A PRACTICAL GUIDE TO MAKING EVERYTHING WORK

**Barry Siskind**

Published in Canada in 2001 by
Stoddart Publishing Co. Limited
895 Don Mills Road, 400-2 Park Centre,
Toronto, Canada M3C 1W3

Published in the United States in 2002 by
Stoddart Publishing Co. Limited
PMB 128, 4500 Witmer Estates,
Niagara Falls, New York, 14305–1386

**www.stoddartpub.com**

To order Stoddart books please contact
General Distribution Services
*In Canada* Tel. (416) 213-1919  Fax (416) 213-1917
Email cservice@genpub.com

10 9 8 7 6 5 4 3 2 1

**Canadian Cataloguing in Publication Data**

Siskind, Barry, 1946–
Bumblebees can't fly: a practical guide to making everything work

1st ed.
ISBN 0-7737-3300-0
1. Common sense.  2. Success — Psychological aspects.  I. Title.
BF637.C5S586 2001     158.1     C2001-900591-1

**U.S. Cataloguing in Publication Data**
(Library of Congress Standards)

Siskind, Barry.
Bumblebees can't fly: a practical guide to making everything
work  / Barry Siskind. — 1st ed.
[128] p. :  cm.

Summary: Promotes the Seven Strategies of Common Sense and
examines how to approach problems to achieve success.

ISBN: 0-7737-33000

1. Common sense.  2. Judgment.   3. Reasoning (Psychology).  4.
Success — Psychological aspects.
I. Title.
153.8   21    2001    CIP

Jacket design: Angel Guerra
Text Design: Tannice Goddard

*We acknowledge for their financial support of our
publishing program the Canada Council, the Ontario Arts Council,
and the Government of Canada through the
Book Publishing Industry Development Program (BPIDP).*

Printed and bound in Canada

*Common sense (which in truth is
very uncommon) is the best sense I know of;
abide by it; it will counsel you best.*
— LORD CHESTERFIELD

# *Contents*

# *Acknowledgements*

The strategies in this book have been percolating in my brain and taking shape on my computer for the past seven years. During that time, countless people have helped me both openly — with criticism, suggestions, and encouragement — and covertly — through comments and insights they shared in conversation. The complete list of names is simply too long to include, but there are a few individuals I want to mention.

I wish to thank the folks at Stoddart, particularly my machete-wielding editors Don Bastian and Jim Gifford, and also editor Janice Weaver and proofreader Kathleen Richards. Special thank-yous are owed to my chief champion, Roberta Barens, and to Geoffrey Siskind, who offered advice on early versions of *Bumblebees Can't Fly* and made an exceptional contribution to this final edition.

I'd also like to thank Robert Mackwood, Ken Mark, Sandy Robertson, Tom Stirr, Tanis Helliwell, Sarah Davies, F. Stephen Ford, Linda Porter, Joan McKnight, Rav Berg, Karen Berg, and Rabbi Avi Nachmias, as well as the thousands of workshop participants and clients who have over the years helped me find the root of common sense.

As you read *Bumblebees Can't Fly*, you will learn that common sense is something we all have. What that means is that there are countless resources at our disposal to learn from. My most precious resource is my family, Jillian, Geoffrey, Mark, Robert, Cory, Lynda, Carol, Suzanne, and Aidyn. And even though common sense is everywhere, there would be no point in it for me without my life partner, Barbara — thanks.

# Introduction

# FLIGHT OF THE BUMBLEBEE

In the early part of the twentieth century, science pronounced bumblebees aerodynamically incapable of flight. Their ratio of body weight to wingspan is disproportionate, the explanation went, and so bumblebees should not be able to fly.

But despite what science said, bumblebees *can* fly. Flight is the most efficient way for bees to get from their nests to the nearest flowers to gather nectar and back again, so they just do it. It's lucky no bumblebees read science journals; if they did, they would never dare leave the ground again.

When bumblebees ignore science and take off in flight, they're using common sense. We, too, have been blessed with common sense. We use it when the solution to a problem appears so obvious and right that no other course of action seems possible. More often than not, however, we don't fully realize the benefits of our common sense in our everyday life.

But what is common sense? Are some of us favoured with it and others not? And if we don't all use it, what's so common about it?

## What Is Common Sense?

Simply put, common sense is the ability to find the right solution to the right problem at the right time. The "right" solution is the one that works best, the one that is the most straightforward or the easiest to implement. Sounds simple, right? So why is it often so difficult to come up with the proper solution?

The answer is that we don't always understand how to use the common sense we were born with. And because we don't know how to use our common sense, we often confront challenges unprepared. Although early man had to face problems such as famine, pestilence, and predation, we have a host of new (and at times equally dangerous) challenges to confront — the information explosion, the loss of corporate loyalty, environmental decline, occupational specialization, space travel, increasingly powerful media, and globalization, to name just a few. Our children and grandchildren will live in a world radically different from the world we knew as children, and they will encounter new challenges we can't even imagine. The only constant in this ever-changing world is common sense. It's our most valuable — and yet least often used — resource.

In this book, I will show you how to employ the common sense you already have — how to recognize it, harness it, and put it to good use. I've devised several easy-to-learn strategies that will allow us how to live in harmony with each other, run our businesses with integrity and honesty, raise our children with hope for a bright future, and achieve whatever we want to in life. The strategies — which I like to call the Seven Strategies of Common Sense — will give you the power to take charge of your life and control your destiny.

## *The Seven Strategies of Common Sense*

My Seven Strategies of Common Sense do not amount to a universal formula for success (like adding one and one and always getting two). After all, what works for one person may not work for another. But these strategies are a constant. In any given situation, each of us can apply the strategies, make adjustments to allow for variables such as our own cultural and social backgrounds or the specifics of that particular situation, and arrive at a workable solution. The way we interpret and execute the strategies may vary, but the strategies themselves always remain the same.

### Strategy #1: Doubt the Obvious

This strategy helps you broaden your horizons so you can see new solutions to everyday problems.

### Strategy #2: Let Your Reach Exceed Your Grasp

This strategy teaches you to look beyond the everyday and see new possibilities ahead.

### Strategy #3: Know Yourself

This strategy explains that every action is grounded in four life forces — values, intellect, emotion, and experience — and helps you balance those forces.

### Strategy #4: Transform Information into Knowledge

This strategy introduces the underlying principles that will steer your thoughts and actions.

### Strategy #5: Embrace the Unexpected

This strategy teaches you that the instinctive or obvious solution is not always the best solution.

### Strategy #6: Stay on Course

This strategy explains when to backtrack and

when to move forward. It's a sure-fire method of getting you back on course if you lose focus.

## Strategy #7: Don't Be Afraid to Change Horses in Midstream

This final strategy teaches you how to recognize when you are on the wrong path, and how to accept that it's time to start over.

Is there an order to the seven strategies? Yes. Each strategy builds upon the last. If you learn each one fully before proceeding to the next, you will develop a system that will help you make sense of your everyday life.

Somehow, somewhere, we've lost sight of what is really important. So what should we do? Find a way to make the picture complete. The missing piece is common sense. Add a dab of common sense to the palette and a clearer picture will emerge, a distinct image for you to understand and follow.

After a day of flying from flower to flower, getting their work done, bumblebees return to the hive and enjoy the honey. If you follow the Seven Strategies of Common Sense, you too will find the honey at the end of the day.

*Strategy*

**1**

# DOUBT THE
# OBVIOUS

*Between the idea*
*And the reality*
*Between the motion*
*And the act*
*Falls the Shadow.*
— T. S. ELIOT, *THE HOLLOW MEN*

All too often, we feel captive to the world we live in. We convince ourselves that we have no control, no authority. And to avoid seizing that control, we tell ourselves, "You can't fight city hall . . ." or "If it was meant to be . . ." or "That's just the way it is."

In truth, these statements only limit our search for solutions; they absolve us of the need to make changes. The philosopher Albert Camus once said, "At thirty a man should know himself like the palm of his hand." Bertrand Russell claimed, "Real life is, to most men, . . . a perpetual compromise between the ideal and the possible." I believe that these messages of resolve — the suggestion that things are as they are and can't be changed — are among the most damaging we give ourselves. They are powerful words that teach us to accept and embrace our own power-lessness.

This first strategy attacks the idea that there are things in life that simply can't be changed. It is the foundation for the six remaining strategies, and if we don't accept it, none of the other strate-gies will be as effective. It teaches us to question some of our long-held beliefs, and to understand that things aren't always what they seem. If we accept without question everything we're told, creativity cannot thrive. And without creativity, progress grinds to a halt and common sense goes out the proverbial window.

### *Truth versus Myth*

In this world, there are two kinds of truths: real truths and notions that you have convinced your-self are truths. This first strategy of common sense helps you distinguish between the truth and any firmly entrenched beliefs — that is, myths — that limit your ability to use your com-mon sense.

Before you begin to look for the truth, however, you must first understand how preconceived notions can cloud your vision. These notions are often a roadblock to change. If you accept them as truths, you severely limit your chances of harnessing your common sense.

We all know some of these firmly held beliefs: men are strong, women are gentle; hard work is always rewarded; governments will protect us; call the police if you're in trouble. Sometimes these beliefs can be misleading. Not everyone who is supposed to be good and trustworthy, for instance, actually is. The system isn't always foolproof. And sometimes blind faith can lead to complacency and even disaster — innocent people end up wrongfully imprisoned; established companies suddenly go bankrupt; seemingly solid relationships fall apart.

So what is truth and what is myth? Take a moment and look at yourself in the mirror. What do you see? A face: nose, eyes, and a mouth. Is that real? Of course. But is that all there is to you? If you conclude that you are just an assembly of body parts, that's a myth — there is more to you than that. The truth is that you are a complex organism, and most of what you are is hidden from view. But your physical body is the package you present to the world. That's why you feel bad when someone says your nose is too big. Your body represents everything about you — both the tangible and the intangible.

Strategy #1 says you must learn to distinguish the tangible from the intangible, myths from the truth. If you don't challenge the myths you encounter, you will reinforce them. That is how such myths get incorporated into the fabric of your daily life (hence the old expression "Tell a lie often enough and it becomes the truth"). And the more commonplace these myths become, the more absolute they seem. This simple premise becomes the basis for our first strategy.

Here's an example. There was once a successful baseball player who was adored by millions of fans and had an astronomical batting average. He had signed a multi-year, multimillion-dollar contract, and was the toast of the town. But his life had not always been blessed with such success.

In his youth, he lacked self-confidence, even though he was supremely talented. But one day, he met a young woman who had been admiring him from a distance. She gave him a medallion on a chain and asked him to wear it around his neck for luck. The first game he played wearing that medallion was the best game of his life. He and the young woman began seeing each other regularly, and soon she asked him to wear the medallion again. He agreed. Once more he played a spectacular game. He was a star in the making and his confidence soared.

The young ballplayer began to believe implicitly in the power of the medallion; in his mind, wearing it meant winning. This belief was reinforced with each additional win, and eventually it became an obsession so strong that he would never play a game without the medallion. But did it really improve his play?

The answer is yes. The medallion did improve his game, though not because the simple amulet possessed magic powers. No, the necklace improved his game because he believed — a conviction borne of repeated experience — that it, even more than his talent, was the key to his success. Would he have been able to perform just as well without it? The answer to that is no — at least not as long as he continued to believe in its power. If he lost the medallion, would that mean the end of his career? Perhaps. Our ballplayer put his fate in the hands of an illusion rather than an absolute: the fact that he was a talented player.

An episode of the television show *Cheers* provides another example. Sam Malone, the owner of the bar where the show is set and a former major-league pitcher, is a recovering alcoholic. In one poignant episode, a fellow pitcher who's in a slump borrows Sam's lucky bottle cap. When his slump miraculously lifts, he refuses to return it. Sam panics. The cap came off the last bottle of beer he ever drank. He fusses and frets throughout the episode because, like the ballplayer with the medallion, he believes his bottle cap is a talisman, the one thing that prevents him from drinking. Without it, he's convinced he will fall off the wagon.

At the end of the episode, Sam stares intently at an unopened bottle of beer with an opener in hand. He snaps the bottle open, holding the cap in one hand and the beer in the other. This is

Sam's moment of truth, but he realizes that what he needs is another bottle cap — not the bottle. What Sam did with his bottle cap is what we all need to do with those things we have accepted as absolute truths: to step back and re-evaluate them by asking ourselves hard questions.

In effect, this is the guiding principle behind our legal system, where the accused must be proven guilty beyond any reasonable doubt. The defence attorney's job is to look at the evidence of a crime and interpret it in a light favourable to the client. The prosecutor's job, on the other hand, is to gather enough evidence to prove that the accused did in fact commit the crime. The defence attorney and the prosecutor are looking at the same scene, the same crime, the same circumstances, even the same "truth." But where the prosecutor sees guilt, the defence attorney must find reasonable doubt. Each is looking at the same story from an opposite perspective. This example shows how a person's intentions can affect his interpretation of events.

Here's another example. The Canadian Diabetes Association recently reported that 80 percent of those diagnosed with late-onset diabetes also suffer from obesity. Overeating and stress often worsen symptoms to the point that they can become fatal. All those with this disease know this, and so they will usually embark on a careful examination of their daily habits, especially their eating habits. This is often followed by ritualistic weighing of every morsel of food consumed. Every ingredient in every meal is scrutinized to the nth degree. People don't want their condition to get worse, so they do what they must do in order to survive — that's common sense.

But a short time into this regimen, a strange thing often happens. Many diabetic patients, faced with a desire to satiate their cravings, start to make trade-offs. They say, "I can have this and skip something later." Or "I will just cheat a little. After all, I have been good so far." One cheat leads to another, of course, and soon they are back to their old habits and back among the obese 80 percent of diabetics.

So why the change in behaviour? The answer is that there is perhaps some secondary gain that is not being confronted. In this case, people may worry about the loss of an activity (eating) that is related to many of their social and cultural events. "If I change my eating habits," they say to themselves, "I will have no way of socializing with my friends." So a diabetic's need to lose weight ends up conflicting with another need. And as long as intentions and behaviour are at logger-heads, the internal conflict prohibits people from using their common sense. This is also why smokers, to use another example, continue to puff away in spite of irrefutable evidence of the asso-ciated health risks. Many of us never figure this out.

Where does this conflict come from? Well, it

usually arises when our behaviour is based on untrue information. ("There are three sides to every story," the saying goes, "mine, yours, and the truth.") Of course, it's not always easy to determine when information is true and when it is untrue, partly because every situation has more than one interpretation. Are the Rocky Mountains one of the world's most breathtaking wonders, for example? Or are they a place fraught with danger, where avalanches kill and destroy? When we change our minds while disciplining our children, do they see flexibility and a willingness to listen or inconsistency and thus a bad precedent? These are examples of the same information resulting in different interpretations. So which answer is the truth?

So often, the real truth of a situation is only hinted at, revealed "through a glass, darkly." That is why, when you're faced with a difficult predicament, you must look at all the surrounding information (especially any secondary gains) before you act. Unfortunately, when we fail to look beyond the surface, accepting only part of the truth, we limit our possibilities — and our growth.

### The Lesson of Copernicus
This leads us to the downside of this strategy: the risks. When you begin to question commonly held beliefs, you risk ignoring valuable conventional wisdom. And sometimes you may find yourself

the victim of personal scorn, even physical injury.

Back in the early 1500s, the astronomer Nicholas Copernicus turned the scientific world upside down. Until that time, the Ptolemaic theory of a geocentric universe had prevailed. Copernicus changed all that by announcing that the universe was in fact heliocentric — that is, that everything rotated around the sun. Suddenly, the earth was nothing more than a planet spinning around a ball of fire. Copernicus' theory rocked two thousand years of scientific tradition and used mathematics to prove that everyone had it all wrong. His heliocentric model successfully explained astronomical irregularities, and today it is an absolute truth. But Copernicus risked ridicule, ostracization, and even death to advance it.

So what can we learn from Copernicus? He was able to look at the same evidence available to everyone and draw different conclusions — conclusions that have stood the test of time. But he did so at great personal risk. And who knows? Perhaps someday his ideas will seem as primitive to future generations as Ptolemy's did to him.

Through the centuries, others have also braved the storm of challenging traditional thought. Christopher Columbus, Sir Isaac Newton, Charles Darwin, Albert Einstein, Pablo Picasso, and Wolfgang Amadeus Mozart were but a few. The poet Percy Bysshe Shelley claimed that "creative thought derived from the linking of everyday concepts in untried or unusual ways." The author Edward de Bono calls this lateral thinking. In his book *Serious Creativity,* de Bono says that lateral thinking is "very much concerned with possibilities and what might be." When we think laterally, we are looking for different answers. "In this sense," de Bono continues, "lateral thinking has to do with exploration." You must ask the right questions and get the right answers to be able to differentiate between the truth and a myth.

Our failure to ask the proper questions has created many of the major problems of our planet — contamination of our water, air, and soil; loss of animal species; deforestation; the greenhouse effect; holes in the ozone layer; and accumulation of toxic waste. In the 1930s, for example, we introduced chlorofluorocarbons (CFCs) to aid in refrigeration. This was seen as a great advancement, and the world endorsed CFCs wholeheartedly. But no one asked about — or foresaw — the danger CFCs posed to the ozone layer. By the time the problem was uncovered, considerable damage had been done. As with so many of the world's ecological problems, the consequences have been devastating. And yet, if we had only asked some common-sense questions, we might have avoided creating many of these problems in the first place.

Remember our credo: nothing is absolute. Your task is to try to see every side of every situation. This means posing the right questions, gauging when your behaviour is in conflict with your intentions, and recognizing your own agenda. You must accept this principle before you can understand and implement the other strategies outlined in this book.

Of course, sometimes this strategy appears to contradict itself. I mean, there are some things we just know to be indisputably true, right? If you stay under water for too long, for example, you will drown. If you jump out of an airplane without a parachute, you will die. If you press your skin to something hot, you will be burned. These statements must surely be absolutes, and therefore the strategy must be wrong. But what do we say to all those people who have survived drownings, fallen from airplanes and lived to tell the tale, walked on hot coals without getting burned? Once again, nothing is absolute.

Many teachers in the early part of the twentieth century taught their students that mankind could never slip the bonds of earth, that everything that could be discovered had already been discovered, that some diseases were incurable. If all those students had accepted such statements as indisputable truths, they would not have grown into today's scientists and thinkers. There would never have been a space program. We would not have found fossilized life forms on Mars. We would never have had computers and the Internet, and there would have been no new medical discoveries.

Those who claim that there is only one right way to do things are closing the door on other possibilities. These people often limit themselves by their "shoulds": "I should accept this as true because everyone says it is," or "It should be done this way because that's the way it has always been done in the past," or "I should accept my disability because my doctors tells me my condition will never improve." These messages put a powerful brake on our creativity, our understanding, our will to succeed where others have failed. You must avoid them at all costs. Instead, embrace this first strategy: be sceptical, explore new mysteries, and find new ways to bring common sense into your life.

## *Making Sense of Strategy #1*

1. Be sensitive to the word "should." Keep a small notebook handy and mark down every time you include it in one of your sentences.
2. For each item on your list, ask yourself whether the "should" is a truth or a myth. Consider the risks and the benefits of ignoring the "should" message.
3. As soon as you have ten items on your list, substitute an alternative belief for each one. Let's say, for example, that your "should" message was this: "I should stay up all night to finish this report because I won't have time tomorrow at the office and nobody else can do it as well as I can." What are the risks of avoid-

ing this message? Well, someone else may have to complete the report, and that person may not do it as well as you would. But what are the benefits? You will get a good night's sleep and be well prepared for tomorrow's challenges. So what kind of alternative belief can you substitute here? Perhaps you can solicit the help of other staff members, getting them to work on sections of the report and consolidating their labour. That way, you will end up with both a good night's sleep and a comprehensive report.

4. If you repeat these exercises for a few days, you will probably conclude that this first strategy is correct, that there *are* several ways of looking at every situation. Soon you will begin to realize that your abilities are limited only by your beliefs about what is true and what is not true.

## *Conclusion*

If you have come this far and feel convinced that this first strategy is taking you in the right direction, you are ready to move on to Strategy #2.

## Strategy

**2**

# LET YOUR REACH EXCEED YOUR GRASP

*I was seldom able to see an opportunity
until it had ceased to be one.*
— MARK TWAIN

The first strategy showed you that you could be limiting yourself by restricting your field of vision. You learned the importance of looking beyond the surface, of accepting the notion that nothing is absolute. In effect, that strategy taught you to look at "shoulds," to examine them against the risk you take by ignoring them. But it is important not to stop there. To do so would again be to limit your options, in turn reducing your chances of success. You must next learn to search for solutions and ideas that are not immediately apparent.

Sometimes that hidden solution or alternative path eludes you. It may even seem that there *is* no other way to proceed. But you must never give up. This second of our seven strategies states that nothing is unknown, no solution is beyond us if we are willing to push the boundaries and look for answers in new and sometimes unexpected places. Everything you need to know exists somewhere, in some form. You only have to reach out and find what you're after. And to do that, you must first step back and take a good, long look at who you are, at your unique place in the universe.

Every one of us is made up of billions of cells, and every cell contains the entire genetic code of the whole body. Each human being is to the universe what the cell is to each human being. The entire blueprint of the universe, in other words, is contained within each one of us. As a result, when you learn a new concept, you are not really *learning* at all. In fact, you are simply recalling what you already know. Have you ever experienced a kind of déjà vu, a moment when you've slapped your forehead and said, "Oh, I knew that already"? This usually occurs when you're faced with knowledge that resonates deep within your subconscious.

You will probably have the same sensation as you work your way through the Seven Strategies of Common Sense. None of these strategies is new, after all. But you will be amazed by the effect they have when you have learned to implement them all together. It's like being given the combination to a bank vault that holds all the knowledge your mind contains. Just as you need the proper pattern of numbers to make the heavy vault door swing open, so do you need the proper common-sense strategy to unlock the knowledge within your subconscious.

## *Order Out of Chaos*

One concept that seems difficult for people to accept is the notion that there truly is order in the universe. Down through time, philosophers have wrestled with this idea. Determinism, a theory that has preoccupied great thinkers for centuries, posits that every event or action is determined by causes external to the will. Chaos theory, it can be argued, is science's attempt to put determinism into a mathematical model. It holds that small and seemingly insignificant events can sometimes have massive and unpredictable consequences. In effect, it's an attempt to find structure in random, irregular events. These theories, and others like them, are attempts to impose order on what has long been viewed as an utterly disorganized world. Yet it is hard to view the world as ordered when we are faced with seemingly contradictory evidence: innocent people are killed by drunk drivers; businesses flourish one day and fail the next; some people have everything while others live with nothing.

Where is the order in all this injustice? Life sometimes doesn't seem fair.

Well, the reason we so often can't see order in the world is because we base everything on what we see, hear, smell, taste, and feel. But we limit ourselves when we interpret the world only through these five senses. As the philosopher Jean-Jacques Rousseau wrote, "All that I perceive through the senses is matter."

The five senses are tools of interpretation, of course, but we have to be able to understand them in relation to other aspects of the world around us. Here is an experiment that will illustrate my point. Line up three glasses of water. Pour hot (but not scalding hot) water into the first glass, lukewarm water into the second, and cold water into the third. Put your finger into the hot water and keep it there for a few minutes, then take it out and place it into the warm water. The warm water will feel cold. Now put your finger into the cold water, and after a few minutes put it back into the lukewarm water. The warm water now feels hot.

This simple experiment shows us how easily we can be deceived when we rely on only one sense — in this case, the sense of touch — without taking other factors into account. If we had nothing other than these five senses to go by, we would experience profound difficulties whenever we had to make even the smallest decisions. How would we know if the water was hot or cold? If all our decisions are limited by the five senses, we can only conclude that the results must be equally limited.

Understanding life's limitless possibilities is the heart of Strategy #2. This second principle of common sense involves developing a world-view that extends beyond your five senses. You are now moving in the realm of perception.

### The Sixth Sense

Have you ever had the feeling that someone was watching you, only to discover that someone was doing just that? Have you ever reached for the phone a fraction of a second before it rang? But how did you know the phone was about to ring? You may have described this kind of feeling as a sixth sense, but it was an actual thought. And everything begins with a thought — an electrical impulse in the brain.

Every single advancement in civilization — from fire and the wheel to DNA mapping and satellite technology — began with an idea. Albert Einstein, for example, apparently sat quietly in a meadow, visualizing flight along a light beam. Out of this musing came his theory of relativity. And perhaps Isaac Newton really did sit under an apple tree and wonder, "Hmm, why did that fall?"

On a very basic level, Einstein and Newton simply tapped into their own intuition — something you can do as well. Indeed, you must understand your intuition before you can access your common sense and unlock the secrets of our second strategy. Simply put, intuition is a means of perceiving something independent of any reasoning process. We are all capable of intuition, to varying degrees. And since we all have the ability, we can all extend our experience of the world beyond our five senses to include this sixth one.

Actors rely on their intuition to create a rapport with their audience. Intuition tells them how the audience members are responding, and how strongly they are involved in the play and its characters. An investor sometimes relies on "gut instinct" to decide which investment decision is the right one. A doctor who applies a lifetime of medical knowledge to a situation may still experience moments when a course of action is based on "feel." Parents constantly rely on their intuitions to determine what is best for their children.

While empirical evidence comes from the environment around us, intuition comes purely from the inside, from our inner minds. Intuition is an internally generated awareness, a form of energy that you can tap into anytime it's needed. But if this energy is all around us, why do some people not see the obvious answers until after the fact? Many of us have experienced the sensation Mark Twain alludes to in the quotation that opens this chapter. Why? The truth is that although the universe has provided us with a wealth of information, we often ignore it, even resist it. We can stare a solution in the face and still not see it.

There's a story about a cyclist who crossed an international border every day carrying a huge bag. Each day, the border guard would stop him and search the bag, but he could find nothing suspicious. He had no choice but to let the cyclist pedal across the border. He felt sure that the cyclist was up to no good. His instinct told him that the man was smuggling something. But what? This pattern continued for weeks, with the guard growing increasingly suspicious. He always had to let the man go, but his suspicions never left him.

Years later, after the customs official had retired, he met the cyclist in a café. He approached him and asked, "Look, I know you were smuggling all those years, but I was never able to catch you at it. I searched you thoroughly, and I could never find anything wrong. I am retired now and can do you no harm. Please let me retire in peace. Were you smuggling?"

The cyclist replied, "Yes, I was."

With a look of satisfaction, the officer said, "I knew it. But what was it?"

The cyclist smiled, took a sip of his coffee, and then replied, "Bicycles. I smuggled bicycles."

Why, like the border guard in this story, do we so often miss the obvious? Why do we resist information that is staring us in the face? Well, perhaps the obvious is too obvious, too simple. Or perhaps it's too unpleasant or difficult to face. Perhaps, like the border guard, we get too caught up in the details to see the big picture.

Whatever the reason, you will continue to resist the obvious for just as long as you continue to perceive the world exclusively through your five senses. You must learn to advance beyond this by developing and trusting your intuition. Soon, you will become conscious of the limitations of your five senses — and startled by the power of your intuition. Remember, your intuition, although intangible, is just as real as all other forms of energy. Intuition is your ability to tap into the universal energy surrounding you.

Why do we not listen to these truths? Why does the scientist work purely on the assumption that nothing can be accepted as "real" until proven by standard scientific methods? Why do some doctors believe that the only correct way to treat a patient is with traditional medicine? Why do some parents ignore signs of emotional pain or discontent in their children, chalking up bad behaviour to rudeness or impertinence?

The answer is that everyone looks at the world with different vision, through a different colour of glasses, so to speak. There are some who are detail-oriented. Others see the bigger picture. While some focus on specific issues — work, money, family, or recreation — others see themselves as part of a wider landscape. Either way, Strategy #2 forces us to look beyond personal perspectives and develop a trust in intuition.

This does not mean that we all end up at the

same place with the same answers, however. There is often more than one "correct" solution available. For example, we all know that the shortest distance between two points is a straight line, right? Well, if this is so obvious, why do people take different paths to reach the same destination? Why don't we all find the straightest possible line and never deviate from it? One answer could be that the deviations along the route are often more interesting (and more seductive) than following the straight and narrow.

We are all different, and thus we need to experience different things, live different lives. These variations are what make us interesting. Arriving at an answer is not always the point of an exercise. If it was, then the journey itself would be meaningless, except as a means to an end. How sad that would be if this were true. There is more to life than reaching a destination, after all. There's the excitement and wonder of exploration, the surprises you find off the beaten path. And the search for these surprises begins the day you are born.

## The Hierarchy of Needs
Our early lives are simple. As infants, we operate out of common sense. Whenever we are wet or cold or hungry, we cry until someone comes along to help us. We rely fully on the support of a loving parent or sibling. But as we grow and mature, we learn to see life through our own eyes, to take

care of ourselves. We are all constantly absorbing and processing information in our own unique way. As we learn new behaviours and new skills, however, life loses that simplicity. Layers of experience accumulate over time, rendering life complex and often perplexing. Sometimes the real reasons for our behaviour become lost. We forget that basic survival lies at the heart of most every action. Remember Maslow and his hierarchy of needs? He believed that physiological needs such as hunger and thirst have to be satisfied before higher, more sophisticated needs can emerge.

If you want proof, watch a group of infants playing. The simplicity of their vision is amazing. They will put any new toy you give them straight into their mouths. If they need to relieve themselves, they simply do it no matter where they are. They may cry one minute and laugh the next. They live and react in the moment. What happens tomorrow is of no consequence.

As adults, we have moved beyond this purely physiological response to stimuli. But that doesn't mean we have to stop reacting intuitively. Even if we have a wealth of experience to call upon, we can still benefit from trusting our intuition or common sense.

Of course, some of us find it difficult to put our faith in something that isn't based in empirical fact. It may seem like a loss of control. (Abraham Lincoln once said, "I claim not to have controlled events, but confess plainly that events have controlled me.") You must learn to overcome this uneasiness and trust your "inner voice," an instinctive, intuitive voice that will guide you at the exact moment when guidance is what you need most. But that means accepting that no matter how brilliant or perceptive you are, some events simply cannot be predicted or anticipated. You must believe that amid the chaos of everyday life, your inner voice will give you the right answer at the right time.

Still, it is not always easy to act on this inner voice. You may doubt its validity, perhaps, or get distracted by the noise and chatter of the world around you. And there is always that fear of yielding control to the voice. But those who listen to its wisdom are invariably pleased with the results. If you deny or ignore your inner voice, I'm willing to bet that you will find yourself consistently venturing down the wrong path. When you trust it, on the other hand, you will be right more often than you will be wrong. Soon, the odds will be stacked in your favour.

If you're willing to accept the concept of an inner voice, that is enough for now. You will return to it again in Strategies #5 and #7.

## *Making Sense of Strategy #2*

1. In your trusty notebook, record in as much detail as you can a time when your instincts were so strong that you immediately knew the right thing to do.

2. Next, think of a time when the right choice was less obvious. In detail, recount your struggle to decide what to do.

3. Now compare the two stories. In the first example, can you pinpoint exactly what it was that made you certain of your course of action? Did you consider any other alternatives at all, or did you just proceed without a second thought? In the second example, was your final decision the right one? What would have happened if you had chosen a different course of action? Was your inner voice telling you the answer all along? If so, why didn't you accept it right away?

## *Conclusion*

You have already come far in your journey. By understanding and accepting the first two strategies, you have laid the groundwork that will allow you to travel through the rest of this book confidently and openly. You are now ready for your first concrete strategy for change.

*Strategy*

**3**

# KNOW YOURSELF

*Good and bad luck [are] synonym[s], in the great majority of instances, for good and bad judgement.*
— JOHN CHATFIELD

From the first strategy, you learned that *nothing* is absolute. And from the second strategy, you learned that everything you need to know already exists. These first two principles set the stage for the strategies that follow. No further progress can be made until you accept their wisdom. And this next strategy is the first to bring more common sense into your life.

In many ways, your mind is like a computer that filters and processes incoming information. How does it work? Well, imagine you went to a party with a friend. The next day, a third person asked you what the party was like. You talked about the food that was served and the entertainment. Your friend, however, focused on who was there and what they wore. Although you and your friend were both at the same event, you reported on it in entirely different ways. The things you focused on would also have affected your behaviour at the party. You might have disliked the entertainment and therefore had a bad time, while your friend saw lots of people she enjoyed and had a great time. You were both exposed to the same information and behaved differently. Yet can you imagine how boring life would be if everyone behaved in the same predictable fashion?

Imagine that your unique perspective on life is plotted on two complementary axes. The vertical axis represents how you filter incoming information. I call this the Values and Experience (VE) Scale. The horizontal axis represents how you process information, and I call it the Intellect and Emotion (IE) Scale.

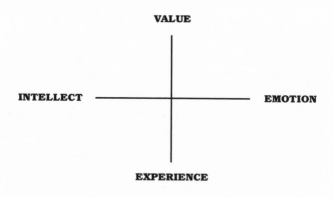

## *The VE Scale*

Strategy #2 taught us that we have access to all the information we need. But what happens to this information next depends on *how* it is filtered. Let's say, for example, that your trusted mechanic tells you your car needs $2,000 worth of repairs. You may or may not decide to get the job done, but you will accept his opinion. If, however, the same information comes from a complete stranger, you will probably view it sceptically and shop around, getting two or three other quotes before you make your decision. In this case, the information is the bad news about your car. Your filter is your relationship with your mechanic.

Every day we are bombarded with information. We accept some of it without question and scrutinize the rest to varying degrees. What do you do when you come upon a park bench with a Wet Paint sign on the seat? Some people will simply avoid the bench, while others will touch it, just to make certain. Maybe the paint has dried, or perhaps the sign is on the wrong bench. Our VE Scale determines the action we take, and this scale is specific to each one of us.

Let me tell you a story about six blind men and an elephant. One after another, each of the six men touched the elephant. The first touched the leg and said, "The elephant is like a tree with a sturdy trunk." The second touched the tail and said, "An elephant is like a rope." The third touched the trunk and exclaimed, "An elephant is like a snake." The fourth touched the ear and said, "The elephant is like a leaf." The fifth touched the elephant's broad side and said, "This animal is like a wall." The sixth touched the tusk and found the elephant to be like a spear. Which of these six blind men was correct? Of course, they were all correct — each from his own perspective. In this case, the information they received was filtered through their sense of touch.

We are exposed to a whole range of sensations and ideas in our lives. These form the basis of our point of view. And once we have adopted this point of view, we often have difficulty keeping an open mind and considering other ways of thinking. Think of our blind men. How would each one try to convince the others that his interpretation was the right one? "For what a man would like to be true," said Francis Bacon, "that he more readily believes." We more easily believe what falls within the scope of our particular viewpoint. We filter information just as a coffee maker filters water through ground coffee: taking out what we want and leaving the rest behind.

So how does our value system come into play? Let's say you're in desperate need of money and someone suggests you rob a bank to get it. What would you do? In all likelihood, you would say no. Certainly none of those who believe in a strong work ethic and have a high degree of personal integrity would choose to rob a bank.

But let us suppose for a minute that you had

been raised by someone who, though kind to you, was a career felon with a value system based on getting whatever he could, by whatever means were at his disposal. For a man like this, the prospect of breaking the law likely wasn't much of a moral dilemma. Would a child growing to adulthood in this milieu have a problem robbing a bank?

In each of these situations, the decision taken rested solely on personal values. Values are instilled in us by our parents (don't steal, get good grades, treat your siblings well); by society (don't hurt your neighbour, obey the laws, don't drive too fast); and by religious organizations (attend regular services, treat others as you would like to be treated). Values become the guiding force behind every decision you make. They can help you make sense of an otherwise confusing world. But when strong-willed people with opposing values clash, conflict arises.

A case in point is the issue of capital punishment. Some people find the very idea of executing people completely abhorrent. But others take more of an eye-for-an-eye approach to justice. Who is right? This type of issue can keep governments vacillating for years. And no matter what decision is made, some group will be upset and angry. Ideally, common sense can be employed to solve these types of dilemmas.

The RIDE (Reduce Impaired Driving Everywhere) program is an excellent example. This program, which originated in Ontario, was designed to curb the number of traffic accidents caused by impaired driving. It gives the police the power to conduct random spot checks and insist on a Breathalyzer test for any driver they suspect has been drinking. The program was an instant success, and traffic accidents caused by impaired driving were substantially reduced. But some murmurs were heard. Could police misuse this power? Was this the first step to a police state? Soon, those who saw the RIDE program in a purely positive light were arguing in court against those who sought to defend personal freedom. Fortunately, Canadian law allows the premise that personal freedom isn't an absolute. "In a free and democratic society," the law reads, "sometimes the benefits outweigh the deleterious effects." A great example of built-in common sense.

This law applies a stringent test that asks if the act and the means to control it provide a greater benefit to society than the lost freedom. The test relies on a firm understanding of the values held in highest regard by (in this case) Canada's citizens.

Unlike values, which (as we saw) are imposed, experiences, the other half of the VE Scale, are acquired. They come from the people you meet; the jobs you hold; your travels, hobbies, or pastimes. They all affect our lives. Here's an example. Someone I know was deeply affected by the death of a friend. The woman, who was in a state of depression, committed suicide by jumping in front of a subway train. She left her two sons and her many caring friends baffled and hurt. The woman I know especially failed to understand the very violence of the act. She knew her friend must have been suffering an anguish far more profound than anyone had realized.

This woman was so affected by her friend's death that she began to change. Shortly afterwards, when she saw an elderly lady struggling with some parcels, she stopped and offered to help. An act of violence and a tragedy had made her a kinder, more caring human being — someone more aware of hardship and its consequences. So what lesson can we learn from this? We are all intertwined, and every action has the potential to change life for all of us. It's all one more ripple in the universal pond.

Let's consider another example of how a person's experiences can influence his behaviour. Prison inmates are meant to experience their time in jail as a deterrent, a discouragement of future criminal behaviour. Instead, the "warehousing" of criminals can have a very different effect. Life in prison is tough, and first-time offenders must learn quickly to use their wits to survive. It is not difficult to see how years of this would make it hard for them to adjust to life outside the prison walls — in a society where violence and crime are not tolerated.

Your life is affected by every experience you have. The instant these experiences occur, you'll undergo some kind of change, perhaps in your mood, perhaps in your awareness of the world around you.

So if our values are at one end of the VE Scale and our experiences are at the other end, then those who are exposed to similar values and experiences must behave in a similar fashion, right? Guess again. Siblings are not all alike in nature, even though they are subject to the same rules, raised with the same values, and share the same home atmosphere and the same parents. They differ in how they interpret those values and experiences. This is why no one can accurately predict how people will turn out.

So now we understand that the information we consume may be constant, but we each filter it according to our VE Scale. This is a good first step. However, there is more to Strategy #3 than values and experiences.

### *The IE Scale*

On the other side of the equation lies the Intellect and Emotion (IE) Scale. If the VE Scale is the filter — that is, how we judge the information we take in — then the IE Scale is the process — the actions that are invoked. It represents how we deal with each bit of information to which we are exposed. And again, we all do this differently.

Each of your decisions is made from an entirely separate standpoint, using different knowledge and experiences. Many of the major decisions you make — buying a house, finding a job, choosing a spouse, or having children — have equally large implications for the rest of your life. Yet you draw on different information for each one.

How do people make their buying decisions? Well, if you want to spend $400 or $500 on a DVD player, you will probably shop around, comparison price, get all the facts together, then decide. But when it comes to buying a house — probably the largest investment most people will ever make — you likely make this decision based simply on emotion. The house you choose may just *feel* right. The beautiful simplicity of the IE Scale is that every decision we make can be plotted somewhere between the emotional and the intellectual.

There are times when you will appear to be acting closer to the intellectual side than the emotional side. The same thing happens with the VE Scale, where you sometimes will be guided more by experience than values. The point at which you make a decision will vary depending on the situation. What's important is that you use these two scales as a guide to understand *how* you reacted. Once this is accomplished, you will have taken a giant step towards understanding common sense. Doing something with this awareness is the second step.

## *The Middle Path Is Often the Best*
It must be understood that true common sense involves a combination of all the forces that guide

us. Values and experiences are extremely important, but so are the intellect and emotions. On
our chart, the ideal point is the centre. This is
the point of the most effective and successful
blending of the factors that influence your deci-
sion- making. Your goal is to see how much closer
to that centre you can move.

Try this experiment. The next time a conflict
arises between you and your spouse or a com-
panion, stop and think. Where does each of you
stand on the awareness scale? Before you can
arrive at an equitable solution, the solution that
makes the most sense to *both* of you, there will
have to be some give and take. The essence of
Strategy #3 is a simple recognition of the com-
promises needed. If each of you can move closer
to the centre by asking the right questions, the
correct solution will seem to jump right out.

The first strategy showed you the importance of
asking the right questions. We can see now that
those questions must uncover enough information to show you how to move closer to the centre.
Here are a few examples:

- Does this remind me of anything I have heard
  before?
- What are the risks of ignoring this information
  and the rewards of acting on it?
- Is this information true or false?
- How do I feel about this?

When you're proceeding through this questioning process, try to avoid "paralysis by analysis." Do not scrutinize things to death. For now, it is enough to understand the VE and IE scales. Trying to look beyond these at this point will only cause confusion.

Let us review what we've learned so far. First, you learned that nothing is absolute. Everything in life can be questioned. Then you learned that there is an answer to everything. All the information we need is available and accessible — it is just a matter of finding it. And now, with Strategy #3, you took some time to analyze what you do when you filter and process information.

## *Making Sense of Strategy #3*

1. Think about your last purchase. Where were you on the VE and IE scales when you decided to buy the item? Would your purchasing decision have been any different if you'd been at a different point on either of these scales?

2. If the item you considered in step 1 was small, repeat the process with a large purchase (a car or a home, for example). Compare your responses for the small and large purchases. How do the VE and IE scales differ for small and large transactions?

3. Now repeat the exercise with a more abstract decision. For example, ask yourself what made you choose your current job. Would your deci-

sion have been any different had you been at a different spot on the VE and IE scales?

## *Conclusion*

You are now well on your way to bringing more common sense into your life. You have been exposed to some new and life-altering information, but it is not enough. Your next job will be to turn this information into knowledge.

*Strategy*

4

# *TRANSFORM INFORMATION INTO KNOWLEDGE*

*Where is the knowledge we have lost in information?*
— T. S. Eliot, *The Rock*

We now know that everything in life can be questioned, and that all the information we need is at our fingertips, waiting to be filtered and processed. Although Albert Einstein is credited with discovering the theory of relativity and Thomas Edison with inventing the light bulb, we could argue that these men simply knew how to process existing information to generate a fresh result. This is not magic; we all have the ability to find the information we need. That is the lesson of the first three strategies.

But sometimes information alone is not

enough. If you had a manual describing how to build a computer, could you do it? Most of us would find the task bewildering. And this raises an important question: what good is information if we are unable to use it? The real challenge lies in transforming information into knowledge, and that is what our fourth strategy is all about.

To gain some understanding of how this next strategy works, think about a simple light bulb. If the positive and negative charges were allowed to connect directly, the bulb would remain dark. A resistor in the form of a filament is used to separate these positive and negative forces; as long as it is there, the bulb can create light. Now think of the electrical current as information and the operational bulb as the effective use of that information (that is, knowledge). The resistor in this case is the link between information and knowledge. Without that link, we would be left with two forces of energy accomplishing nothing. You need the everyday equivalent of these resistors to help you convert the information you receive into knowledge.

The process of converting information into knowledge differs for us all. We each interpret information through our "resistors" in ways that vary dramatically. To illustrate this point, let's consider the game Broken Telephone. In this game, a group of people sit in a circle, whispering a message from person to person. By the time the message has travelled the entire circle, it has usually become unrecognizable. Is this simply a result of poor listening? Or does the message change because each person filtered the information differently?

Here is another example. A boy and a girl are walking in a park on a beautiful day. The sun is shining and a pair of squirrels dash across the footpath, racing each other for the next nut. The boy takes the girl's hand and smiles. From a distance, both sets of parents are watching the scene unfold.

Now imagine what each player in our little tableau is thinking. The girl reflects on how romantic a walk in the park is. The boy is amazed that the girl actually let him hold her hand and wonders if he should try for a kiss. The boy's father is proud of his son's confidence with the girl. The girl's dad is feeling protective. The boy's mother is absorbed with thoughts of losing her son to this other woman. And the girl's mom is imagining her daughter as a beautiful bride. Each of them has his or her own (at times conflicting) interpretation of the same event.

Although our interpretation of events will vary, we are all governed by the same guiding principles. Our resistance to common sense stems from a lack of understanding of the principles by which we make everyday decisions. These principles are the core of who you are. They act as a rudder, guiding you through your sea of possibilities. Once these principles are understood and adopted, your resistance to common sense is lessened.

Three principles — sense of purpose, commitment, and inner strength — form the core of your character. Once you have a firm grasp of how these principles affect you, your life will be defined in ways you had never imagined. You will feel compelled to do what you know is right. No decision that goes against your principles can be taken. Let's consider each one in turn.

### *Sense of Purpose*

The first guiding principle is *sense of purpose.* This is a consciousness of who you are and where you are going. Most people never develop a clearly defined sense of self. They wander aimlessly through life without direction or purpose. Why is this? Well, many simply don't bother — or perhaps don't know how — to take a step back and create a long-term plan for their lives. So often, people choose — by default or intent — to leave their destiny in the hands of others rather than taking control themselves.

But how can you create a life plan when the world around you is constantly changing? Corporations are downsizing, and you can never be sure how your job will change — or even whether you will continue to have a job. Your children are growing beyond recognition, and you perhaps feel a need to redefine your relationship with your spouse. Technology is changing so rapidly that you cannot keep up. What are you going to do? What do you want to achieve in the long term? What is the point of achieving anything when there are no guarantees?

I knew a man who planned his life very carefully. But he knew that all his dreams and plans were useless without good health. So he adopted a healthy lifestyle, eating sensibly and exercising five or six times a week. He was fit and strong, and when he suffered a fatal heart attack at the age of forty-eight his friends and colleagues were shocked. It might seem that he planned in vain, that he had squandered all that time and energy. But those who were closest to him were certain that he would not have lived his life any other way. He lived forty-eight years to the fullest, and not a day was wasted. Not many of us can say the same.

With a sense of purpose, you can take control of your destiny, instead of leaving it in the hands of others. But as my late friend learned, there are no guarantees. If your purpose is to acquire material things and nothing more, you are wasting your time. You will have no control over loss from wars, tornadoes, fire, flood, and other acts of God. Even losing your job or getting divorced can easily wipe out your possessions — and your dreams.

If you take control of your destiny, at least your fate is more or less in your own hands. Gen. Douglas MacArthur once said, "There is no security on this earth. Only opportunity." You must learn to make the most of the opportunities that present themselves.

Of course, there also must be an element of realism in your long-term plans. There is no point in planning to become a great dancer if you do not have the correct body type. Many young people, on reading Ayn Rand's *The Fountainhead*, dream of studying architecture, of designing buildings that will define civilization itself. But it helps if you are able to draw! Dreams in themselves are not always enough.

Sometimes, defining your sense of purpose means facing some difficult questions. Is there life after death? Is there a God? What does the universe hold for me? How can I contribute something of value to the world? Unless we ask these questions, we will never find our true purpose, and common sense will remain evasive. We ignore them at our peril.

One man I know had the courage to ask these questions. After doing a lot of soul searching, he developed a personal mission. "My purpose in life is to be an 'opportunity provider,'" he said. "I pride myself on being able to help my employees and family find creative and intelligent solutions. I take some credit for this because I think I have a real gift for creating an environment in which people grow. It is very useful in my roles of father, husband, employer, and friend. Before I added the title of 'opportunity provider,' all these other roles were not well defined for me. Now I have injected real meaning into each role I play in life.

"What it takes to be a good father was always fairly clear to me. But the more I learned, the more I had to learn. . . . By adding [the role of] 'opportunity provider,' I was able to define more clearly the type of father I wanted to be. . . . I am still there for my children, but when a problem presents itself, rather than solving it for them, I ask questions and help them to seek solutions for themselves. Each challenge they face becomes an opportunity for me to help them develop the skills they need to handle life on their own. . . . As an 'opportunity provider,' I live my life looking for ways to use my talents to give others more chances to develop their own abilities."

Many people go through their lives taking whatever they can, giving little or nothing in return. But only those who take and give back complete the circuit of universal energy. They tend to lead fuller, more meaningful lives. The secret of making the universal energy work for you is to give back *more* than you take out. Defining your sense of purpose gives you the tools you will need to complete the universal circuit, just like our "opportunity provider." But defining your sense of purpose takes time, energy, and the will to succeed. It means examining all your strengths and weaknesses, talking to people and really listening to what they have to say. Part of that search involves listening to your inner voice, the voice you first learned about in Strategy #2.

## *Commitment*

The second guiding principle is *commitment.* A sense of purpose brings with it certain obligations. And unless you plan to live alone in a cave, your sense of purpose will always affect others. Once you have defined who you are, you will begin to live in a certain way. People will come to expect particular attitudes and behaviours from you. These attitudes and behaviours are the standards implicit in your chosen role, and they cannot be denied. There will be times when the going gets tough, when you will be tempted to stray. To combat this temptation, you must make a commitment to live according to these standards every day.

Sadly, there are countless stories of people not living up to the standards of their chosen roles: priests, police officers, judges, doctors, teachers, and so on. The priest who betrays a confidence, the policeman who frames the innocent, the judge who sentences without mercy, the doctor who takes dangerous shortcuts, the teacher who abuses her authority — all are clearly failing to fulfil their commitments, and in doing so, they fail those around them. Unless you are willing to make a firm commitment to take on the obligations connected with your new role, there is no point in attempting the exercise in the first place.

I had a friend who was a workaholic. Ray was utterly focused on his career, often to the exclusion of his friends and even his family. Then he had a cancer scare. This brush with mortality caused him to reassess his life and re-order his priorities. Ray decided he would be a happier, more fulfilled person if he focused less on his job and more on the people around him.

One day, Ray was running late for an appointment. On the way there, he came across a homeless man who seemed to be in some distress. The old Ray would have ignored the man and carried on his way. Making his appointment would have been his top priority. But the new Ray stopped and offered assistance, even calling for help on his cellphone. Missing the appointment, he knew, was probably going to cost him some business. But he also understood that he had redefined his role in life, and that his new role came with obligations to put the needs of others ahead of his own.

As Ray discovered, once you have set your course, staying on it can be difficult. The path is littered with roadblocks and unexpected diversions. But as long as you maintain a clear image of who you are, these are nothing more than simple detours. It may take you a little longer to get where you are going, but the destination remains the same. Your sense of purpose and the standards you set determine the path you will follow and the actions you will take. They will govern how you bring order, a sense of meaning, and common sense into your life. But what happens when you make a wrong choice? Do you still stay committed?

Here is a story I heard recently that addresses this situation. John was a trusted employee. He was also a personal friend of Hugh, the boss. He was given every opportunity to succeed — more opportunity, perhaps, than was afforded other employees — because his boss had two roles to fulfil: employer and friend. When Hugh found out that John had been stealing from him, he was uncertain which standards should prevail. As a friend, he had a measure of empathy for John's personal situation. But as a businessman, he knew that John had options other than stealing. In the end, John was fired and the friendship between the two men suffered.

This incident greatly affected Hugh's personal goals and attitudes. "My sense of purpose," he stated, "is to find ways to help people cope better with their lives. One tool to accomplish this goal has been to create and run a successful business . . . built around my vision and sense of purpose. Having employees that steal is not in any way beneficial to the fulfilment of this vision. A conflict arose because I tried to be both a friend and an employer. But the two have different standards. There are going to be conflicts. As an employer, [I had] no choice but to terminate the business relationship with John. As a friend, [I had] an obligation to help John get his life back on track."

Hugh's experience shows that circumstances can sometimes change in such a way as to cause you to re-examine your sense of purpose. Is it still valid? Do the standards still apply? If you choose the wrong path or your sense of purpose is no longer valid, you must make a change. A wise man once said, "If you find you are digging yourself into a hole, throw away the shovel." When we get to Strategy #7, you will learn when to make this change. But first, let's look at our third principle, *inner strength.*

## *Inner Strength*

You will need inner strength on a day-to-day, minute-to-minute basis if you want to be able to fulfil your commitment to the standards set by your sense of purpose. You will be faced with a persistent temptation to compromise your values. Your inner strength will serve as a constant guide, a moral compass that will keep you steadfast in your resolve.

But remember that inner strength was also part of our third strategy. There we learned the importance of a firm understanding of how you look at things now and how far you have to move to get to the centre of the IE and VE scales. This can be a gut-wrenching experience, and it may mean challenging your core beliefs. But if you face up to some harsh truths about yourself, the experience will be invaluable.

I had a friend who was dying of complications from diabetes. He was in constant pain, and his life was made bearable only with morphine. This hard-working family man with two children and six grandchildren had always faced life bravely and honestly. He knew his strengths as well as his limitations, and his mantra was "You have to play the cards you were dealt." In his final months, despite his pain, he still found the energy to smile and greet each child or grandchild warmly whenever they came to visit. He showed great inner strength, even as he was dying. He played the cards he was dealt without complaint or regret.

You can frequently find similar stories in the biographies of well-known people. Too often, their accomplishments came only at great personal cost. And many had personal demons that threatened to defeat them at every turn. There's nothing unusual in this. We all have imperfections, and all the common sense in the world will not eliminate them. As the biographer Norman Cousins once said, "The essence of man is imperfection."

Successful people make mistakes. But the truly successful are usually those who find the inner strength to pick themselves up and try again. These are the people who are not afraid to choose a new career or get help when they need it. When they stumble, they confront their demons, restore their inner strength, and try once again to be the kind of people they want to be.

I once heard the actor Paul Newman speak of his years as a young star. When he was asked what he sees when he watches his old movies, he answered, "I see an actor who worked too hard." Perhaps he was trying to find himself in those years. Now that he's into his seventies, he realizes that he no longer has to try as hard to develop his roles. He found his inner strength, and he seems more content. A lot of successful older people exude this inner peace. It says, "I am who I am, and I am where I want to be."

Still, reaching this point in your own life can be difficult. You will exercise bad judgment at times and make mistakes along the road. You need to learn to view those mistakes as learning opportunities. Walt Disney was once quoted as saying, "My bankruptcy at a young age was a great teacher." After repeatedly failing to invent the light bulb Edison said, "Now I know one thousand and one ways not to build a light bulb." The astute see the opportunity for learning in every mistake and adjust their future behaviour accordingly. Those who lack inner strength repeat the same mistakes over and over, then wonder why their lives never change.

A homeless man once shared a hot dog with me on the steps of a downtown Toronto office building. He described for me how he saw some of his homeless friends struggling to survive while others simply gave up the fight. Listening to him, I suddenly realized that we were not that different. Certainly I had more safety nets waiting to catch me if things went wrong: personal savings, friends and relatives who would help me, even government assistance. This man and his friends were engaged in a more obvious life-or-death fight, but at heart we are all struggling to survive.

Most of us have moved up Abraham Maslow's hierarchy of needs, of course, and as a result we ignore our primary requirements until we are faced with losing everything. The media is filled with stories of people who suffer near fatal accidents and vow to change their lives. Terminally ill patients wonder why they wasted precious moments, days, years on things that suddenly seem trivial. The punchline of a famous joke I once heard claims that no dying man's last words are "I wish I had spent more time at the office."

These people have been handed a gift, a reminder that the urge to survive is at the heart of everything we do. This simple, almost childlike view of life will allow you to shed the layers of experience that sometimes cloud your sense of purpose. If you make a commitment and realize your inner strength, your resistance to common sense will be greatly diminished.

## *Making Sense of Strategy #4*

1. Turn back to your notebook and make a list of all the roles you play in your life (parent, worker, friend, spouse, etc.).
2. Beside each role, enumerate the strengths you bring to it.
3. Compare the final lists to see if some strengths show up for more than one role. Ask yourself, "If I can contribute this strength to those around me and use it to guide my life, will it be a satisfying experience?" Think about your answer before you write it down. Those strengths you feel are important will help you define your sense of purpose.

## *Conclusion*

Strategy #4 takes time to absorb and implement. You need to let the information in this chapter percolate through your mind before you try to put it into practice. And when you begin to apply it, you will likely find that not everything in your life is as it should be. When this happens, you will need to invoke our next strategy.

*Strategy*

**5**

# EMBRACE THE
# UNEXPECTED

*The heart of man is made to reconcile
the most glaring contradictions.*
— DAVID HUME

So what have we learned so far? The first two strategies taught us that nothing is absolute and that everything we need to know is at our disposal. The third strategy explained how we filter and process information, and the last strategy introduced the three guiding principles that will help us transform information into knowledge.

So now you are ready for this fifth strategy. In today's world, things are not always what they seem. This next strategy addresses this inconsistency and suggests ways of finding solutions in unexpected places. Let's consider an example.

A simple, unassuming man once changed the world. Without raising a sword or firing a shot, he became a leader whose name still resonates a half-century after his death. His people lived in a country that was governed by a powerful nation — a nation whose strength had created an empire that reached to every corner of the globe. When the first rumblings of dissent were heard, the empire struck back, sending the world's best-equipped army to quell any uprising. But the natives numbered in the hundreds of millions and the troops only in the tens of thousands, so the obvious solution would have been to organize them and drive the intruders into the sea. These were hundreds of millions of illiterate people, however, and they had neither the expertise nor the resources to mount such a counteroffensive. Their leader saw only a bloodbath ahead, so he decided on the opposite approach: instead of fighting war with war, he chose to fight war with peace. Through his peaceful protests, he was able to draw international attention to the plight of his people and force the empire to withdraw.

Mahatma Gandhi understood that sometimes answers lie not with the obvious, but with the unexpected. There is *always* more than one solution to every problem, and often the one with the best fit is the most surprising.

Strategy #5 is based on science. Isaac Newton claimed that for every action, there is opposed an equal reaction. This holds true for the human experience as well. The astute person recognizes reactions that occur in nature and looks in the opposite direction to make sense of things — just as Gandhi did.

From the point of view of the people of colonial India, British imperialism meant oppression, and the natural impulse was to resist. We could even argue that the British presence created the potential for violence. There was a cause-and-effect relationship, in other words. It's important for us to recognize such relationships, for we must get to the heart of any situation before we can apply common sense. But don't be deceived. Sometimes, the more you are drawn into the cause-and-effect debate, the further away from a common-sense solution you travel.

As confusing as this sounds, it goes to the heart of this strategy. What seemed like the right solution can sometimes turn out to be wrong because you have misinterpreted the cause-and-effect relationship by placing blame in the wrong corner. Each person believes his own perspective is the right one. The author Richard Bach once wrote, "What the caterpillar calls tragedy, the master calls a butterfly." When you're trying to make sense of your own life, remember that the only relevant viewpoint is your own.

## *Reversing Cause and Effect*
My friend Terry was an administrative assistant to the president of a large multinational conglom-

erate. Last year, she went through a painful separation after Bob, her partner, left her for another woman. Betrayed and angry, Terry was consumed with thoughts of revenge, spite, even violence. These thoughts soon overwhelmed her, affecting every corner of her life. Friends began to avoid her. Her family lost patience. Her work suffered badly.

From Terry's point of view, Bob's leaving caused her anger. Her negative response was simply the effect. She felt herself a victim of events, powerless and weak. The more she allowed her anger to overtake her thoughts, the deeper the despair she felt.

Many people assume, as Terry did, that there is a logical progression from cause to effect — Bob dumped Terry, and therefore Terry is miserable. But life does not always flow from a cause to a corresponding effect. Sometimes, to take control you must reverse the process. In this way, you can regain command of events taking place around you. This is the lesson Terry needed to learn. In fact, her anger was the cause and her unhappiness the effect. She needed to realize that *she* was the cause of the outcome, and therefore that *she* had to take control of the situation and make sense of it. When we turn things around in this way, we can see that often the opposite answer makes common sense. This is the essence of this next strategy.

## Exercising Strategy #5

There are three basic steps to exercising Strategy #5: reverse the progression, visit the desired outcome, and articulate your intentions. Let's examine each of these in turn by using the example of a hardware superstore that was planned for the heart of Ontario's cottage country.

Recently, this well-known franchise bought land that was strategically placed to allow the store to serve a half-dozen small towns that already had ten to twelve stores providing building supplies, hardware, and lumber. A boom in vacation real estate had brought a staggering number of new cottage owners, and the franchisees felt certain there was a burgeoning market for businesses focused on home improvement.

As soon as plans for the store were announced, the local business owners were incensed. "It will take all our customers away," they moaned. "It will kill downtown traffic. Woe are we." From their point of view, the cause of their problems was the mammoth store. The effect was the exodus of customers they were certain they would see. No matter how they approached the situation, they could reach only one conclusion: they faced doom at the hands of that mammoth store. The business owners needed to invoke Strategy #5 and turn 180 degrees for a new and better perspective.

- ### Step 1: Reverse the Progression
  To exercise this strategy, the first step is to

reverse the progression and regain some control over the situation. Our hardware and
lumber merchants needed to stop blaming the
giant store for their troubles and begin accepting responsibility themselves. In truth, the
warehouse store was the *effect,* not the cause.
For some reason, the loyalty of their customers
was being outweighed by their need for con-
venient one-stop shopping. Before they could
begin to combat the superstore, they needed to
ascertain why their customers were proving
disloyal.

- ### Step 2: Visit a Desired Outcome
  Clearly, the goal of the local merchants was to
  stay in business. But they had become com-
  placent. They were comfortable with their
  customer base, and they made little or no effort
  to find out if they were really providing the
  products and services their customers wanted.
  When they began asking themselves if there
  were other products or services their customers
  would like, they realized that they didn't know
  how their customers would respond. Although
  they had thought they knew their customers
  well, that turned out to be far from the truth.

- ### Step 3: Articulate Your Intentions
  The next step was to devise a plan of action.
  The merchants wanted to stay in business, but
  they now understood that the status quo was

not an option. So they began asking themselves what they had to offer and what their customers wanted. Soon they were surveying customers, forming buying groups, and satisfying niche markets. The threat of the big-box store had woken them up and forced them to re-engage with their old customers and go out in search of new ones. Instead of facing bankruptcy and the death of the downtown shopping area, they found new life in the lessons of Strategy #5.

## A Few More Success Stories

So how did our three-step program work for Terry? Well, once she realized that her anger, not Bob, was the source of her unhappiness, she was able to reverse the progression. She then visited a desired outcome — to be happy in her new life without Bob — and thus she was able to move on and begin to look for a new relationship that would satisfy her needs in ways that the one with Bob had not.

Let's consider another example. A young entrepreneur I knew once admitted that it was very difficult for him to trust other people. He constantly saw better or more efficient ways of doing things, and he never hesitated to correct subordinates. "Nobody can do this as well as I can," he would tell himself as justification for looking over everyone's shoulders. When business got slow, he would push. When people failed to perform, he would push. When he needed new ideas, he would push.

But all this pushing was a symptom of a greater problem: his inability to trust others. He simply did not trust his staff to do the jobs they were paid to do. Fortunately, he became acquainted with Strategy #5, and he realized that with a different approach, he might just be able to solve his problem. He first reversed the progression by learning to view *himself,* not his allegedly incompetent staff, as the cause of his stress. He then resolved to run a business that would produce results without his constant interference. His chosen course of action was to let go rather than push. And he soon began to let his people work at their own speed, and in their own way, with less interference. Almost immediately, a fresh creativity began to flow and his business started to improve. This entrepreneur was able to invoke Strategy #5 by removing his blinkers and learning to trust.

Here is another example. *The Horse Whisperer* is a wonderful book by Nicholas Evans. It tells the story of Annie, who is trying to help her daughter deal with the effects of an accident while searching for understanding in her own life. Towards the end of the book, Annie has to choose between moving to Montana and leaving her family behind or returning to her life as she knew it. When she tells her husband, Robert, that she needs some time to think, he says, "Take as much time as you like, but don't come home unless you really want to." Robert is clearly exercising Strategy #5. He reversed the progression by placing responsibility for the success of the marriage on Annie's shoulders rather than his own. His stated intention is to let her decide what she wants, and his course of action is to wait. Another husband might have insisted that his wife return or threaten divorce, but Robert handles it by placing on her the burden of her own freedom.

Strategy #5 can also apply to your personal financial planning. If you own mutual funds, you know (or you should know) that they are long-term investments. But if the market drops sharply, your knee-jerk reaction might be to sell and cut your loses. The cause is a drop in the market and the effect is your bailout. But if you remember that you're investing long term, you should be buying rather than selling. The cause is now a market opportunity and the effect is your decision to buy. If your assumption of long-term growth was correct in the first place, future market increases will result in even greater profit.

## The Four Stages of Knowledge

Like Strategy #4, this strategy requires some time and patience to master. You must take the information you have just acquired, process it, and transform it into knowledge. The process is similar to our path to learning, which passes through four distinct stages. In a nutshell, these are:

**Stage 1: The unconscious incompetent.** At this stage, you don't have enough information to solve your problems, and you don't even understand that you don't have enough information.

**Stage 2: The conscious incompetent.** At this stage, you still lack the information, but you now see the need to fill the information gap.

**Stage 3: The conscious competent.** You now have the information you need and are aware you have it, but you are still unsure of how to use it.

**Stage 4: The unconscious competent.** You have the information and have internalized it to the point that you don't have to think about the details to know what works and what doesn't. You have successfully converted information into knowledge.

I saw this process in action when I decided to take up tennis. I thought it was something easily mastered, so I went with a partner to the courts in the local park. This was stage one, the unconscious incompetent. I couldn't serve properly, returning the ball was truly hit-and-miss, and most of my time was spent retrieving tennis balls from the surrounding property. Help was needed, and that led me to stage two, the conscious incompetent. Lessons with a professional teacher were in order.

The lessons with the professional were helpful,

and I learned some of the basic moves: how to stand, how to hold the racquet, and how to hit the ball. But I soon became so tied up concentrating on stance and movements that I felt I would have been better off knowing nothing. I was now a conscious competent.

Sensing my frustration, the professional told me to be patient. With a lot of practice, I would be able to make my movements automatic. He promised a greatly improved game, and he was right. I grew to be . . . well, at least an unconscious competent.

Those grappling with the notion of common sense and the lesson of Strategy #5 undergo the same process. The three steps put you in the category of the conscious competent. The next challenge is to move to stage four — the unconscious competent. This is the point at which information has been converted into knowledge, and it's the point when you will be able to come up with common-sense solutions without thinking everything through step by step. You will have learned to trust your intuition.

### Hearing Your Inner Voice

Remember the inner voice you first learned about in Strategy #2, the place in your mind where only the truth is spoken? This is the equivalent of having a powerful processor in your brain. Once it has been programmed properly, it acts instantly. No longer do you have to progress through each lesson step by step. Instead, each situation that presents itself is met by both a lifetime of stored information and the processing structure you have learned.

This inner voice is a gentle voice that guides you in your everyday decisions. Even if the voice tells you to do something that seems to defy logic or contradict what you believe, you must learn to trust it. If it says that some information is still lacking and you do not yet know how to act, you must revisit the three guidelines of this strategy. And if you ignore it, you do so at your peril.

Strategy #5 is elegant in its simplicity. At heart, it tells you that if you stop analyzing things to death and avoid getting bogged down in unproductive detail, real progress can be made. It tells you to trust your inner voice, even when to do so seems to defy logic. This will eliminate the conscious need to stop and figure out cause and effect.

This strategy is one of the toughest to accept, and you will most assuredly backslide from time to time. It may prove difficult to resist the urge to intellectualize, to spend hours playing mind games or attempting to guess the motivations of other people. Your best course of action when this happens is simply to go with it. Experience is the greatest teacher, after all, and you will learn the most from the mistakes you make. Your indulgence will only reinforce this strategy.

## *Making Sense of Strategy #5*

1. In your notebook, describe a situation when you felt out of control or were a victim of circumstances. Don't analyze this yet — just set the scene as you remember it.
2. When you reread your description, attempt to determine cause and effect.
3. Next, relive the situation (in your mind) using the three steps you learned in this strategy: reverse the progression; visit a desired outcome; articulate your intentions.
4. Describe your reaction to this situation now. Determine how Strategy #5 might help you develop healthier, more productive solutions to situations like the one you've just analyzed.

## *Conclusion*

In the beginning of this book, you read about the widely held opinion that no one can learn common sense — you either have it or you don't, says the theory. But Strategy #5 proves that with practice, you too can be one of those self-assured people who always has a solution that makes sense. Don't charge ahead too quickly yet, however. You now need to learn that making sense and being right are not always the same thing, and that a belief that every action is the right one will lead to failure and frustration. That is why you need our next strategy.

*Strategy*

**6**

# STAY ON COURSE

*Life can only be understood backwards;*
*but it must be lived forwards.*
— SØREN KIERKEGAARD

I deally, we would choose the right course of action in every circumstance. Instead, we often find ourselves acting without really knowing whether we have made the correct, common-sense move. Usually we discover the flaws in the path we have chosen only after the fact. Why is this? Well, it's most often a result of either lack of experience or faulty information. This next strategy forces us to re-examine what happened when the results of our actions were inconsistent with our intentions.

Picture this. On a typical morning, you are in a

hurry, getting ready to leave for work. You quickly gather everything you need — briefcase, coat, umbrella, keys . . . KEYS! Your keys are missing. Because you're a creature of habit, you always leave them on a ring beside the front door, but now they're not there. You look everywhere, but without luck. Before you know it, you're late for work.

After taking a moment to breathe deeply to prevent a stream of scatological or profane utterances escaping your mouth, you begin to go over everything you did from the moment you last saw the keys. You parked your car, unlocked the front door, came into the entry hall, put your briefcase down, took off your coat, said hello to your family, went into the kitchen, and sat down for dinner. By retracing your steps like this, you can narrow your search and perhaps even jog your memory. All of a sudden, you remember your son asking if he could borrow the car. You told him where the keys were, and of course he failed to return them to their rightful place. Now you can shift your search from finding the keys to finding your son. This is an excellent example of how common sense can help us out of a frustrating experience. Whether you are trying to find a lost article or close a business deal, this next strategy can be of tremendous value.

### Keep It Simple
In the case of the lost keys, it was easy for you to

find your starting point. You simply went back to the last time you saw the keys. But the search for answers to more difficult questions can lead you into a quagmire of detail. Often we make things worse ourselves by overcomplicating them.

Common sense says the place to start when you want to realign your actions is the point at which you last experienced success. If you have ever been fishing, you will understand this. Perhaps you have been out on a lake and spotted a fellow angler. When you pull your boat alongside his, you see that he has had some success.

"Looks like you've been lucky," you say to him.

"Not bad," he agrees. "Look at this." He holds up a ten-pound northern pike.

"Where did you catch that?" you ask.

The successful fisherman now provides a detailed description of the place and method of his great catch, and you speed off to find the spot, forgetting one important detail: no fisherman will tell you truthfully where he made a catch, because he does not want you fishing at his spot. So as you go off on the wrong track, you leave him grinning and reeling in another massive pike.

To find your starting point, you have to ask the right questions. The fisherman in our example asked the wrong one. If he had said, "Do you mind if I fish alongside you for a bit?" his fellow sportsman probably would not have been churlish enough to refuse. The two men might even have got friendly and found they had many things in common. Perhaps the successful fisherman would even have been willing to share advice on lures or a different casting technique. Soon they might both have filled their boats with pike.

When you read our first strategy, you learned that the failure to ask the right questions can create major problems in your life. The right questions are those that help you understand how and why you took certain actions. And the answers to these questions, as we have just seen, can be uncovered through this new strategy. It all starts with a plan of action.

Every entrepreneur knows that a strategic plan is crucial to the success of his business. Such a plan will anticipate all possible pitfalls and develop strategies to handle or avoid them. It will focus on areas such as sales, marketing, finance, administration, and product development, and it will likely include checkpoints where the manager can stop and evaluate the progress made. An astute manager will not wait until a project is complete before assessing its potential for success.

You must develop a strategic plan for your own life. This plan will include predetermined points where you can stop and measure your success and make adjustments if things are slowing down or problems have cropped up. You should review your plan on a regular basis and rely on your new-found common sense to determine when to carry on and when to change course.

With the lost keys, the starting point — the last time you remember seeing them — was obvious. And that made it easy for you to retrace your steps and find success. If you had not found the answer so quickly, however, your strategy should then have been to review your actions in an ascending order of detail. For the first round, you would have picked the bigger events such as parking your car, coming through the front door, hanging up your coat, greeting your family, and so on. But if these big events didn't lead you to your keys, you would have gone on to the next level of detail: you walked through the front door and across the hall to the closet, hung up your coat on the wooden hook on the left side of the cupboard, talked to your son about his day and his need for the car, walked into the kitchen and tripped on a piece of loose carpet, said hello to your wife and smelled the aroma of fresh garlic in the pot of pasta sauce on the stove, etc.

If you *still* did not have the clue you needed, you would have carried on to the next level of detail, and eventually you would have found your keys. It's very important that you increase the amount of detail only when you need to, thus eliminating the possibility of getting bogged down with irrelevant information.

Interestingly, the detail you add generally relates to one of your five senses. Look back to the example above. In the first stage, all the detail is largely visual: you imagine yourself parking your car and greeting your family. But as the detail increases, you begin to call on some of your other senses: you feel the wooden hook on which you hung your coat; you hear your son asking for the car; you smell the garlic in the pasta sauce. You can see how much more powerful your memory becomes when you also involve those other senses.

Now, you may be thinking back to our second strategy and wondering if I have forgotten what I taught you there. You're probably asking yourself, Didn't he tell us that we limit ourselves when we interpret the world only through our five senses? But I don't believe there's any contradiction here. The world we live in is a sensual one, and the easiest first step to invoking Strategy #6 is to go back to your five senses. If you still can't find your keys even with all the additional detail, that's the time to sit back and let your intuition do the work.

When you are calling on your five senses, be sure to select your sensual memory according to what works best for you. Start with the sense you use most, in other words. If you recall things best by visualizing them, then sight should be your first level (as in the example of our lost keys). But how else do you examine your world? When you see flowers, do you enjoy their scent or their colour? Do you recall the taste of a good meal, or did the conversation around the table make a bigger impression? To create your personal list, think back to certain events in your life and determine how you remember them. Add one sense at a time as you increase the detail.

The right questions to ask yourself when you're recreating any event are those that help you to capture the proper amount of detail. "How did the kitchen smell? What noises did I hear? How did I feel when I got home?" These are the kinds of things that will help you retrace your steps accurately. Imagine waking up slowly from a deep sleep. Perhaps the smell of coffee brewing in the kitchen is what you first sense. Then you become aware of a breeze tickling your face from an open window, the smoothness of the sheets on your skin, a bird singing in the backyard, and so on. You will have the same sense of coming to full consciousness as you add detail to whatever event you are trying to recreate. At some point, you will be able to stand back from your completed picture and say to yourself, "Why didn't I see that the first time?" This is the beauty of Strategy #6.

Let's consider another example. Jake and Mary divorced a number of years ago. It was a long, bitter divorce, but as hard as it was for both of them, it was even harder on Heather, their daughter. Like many children, she felt responsible for the breakup of her parents' marriage. She would often say, "If I hadn't been so demanding . . ." or

"If only I . . ." The whole situation was extremely difficult for the young girl. Common sense should have told Heather that she bore no responsibility for the situation between her parents, but she was unable to see this for herself. All the facts became confused in her mind.

Fortunately, Jake and Mary were astute enough to recognize this, and they immediately sought professional help for their daughter. The therapy made it possible for her to understand what had happened. Heather was able to go back to a point when her family was in harmony and then move forward to recall incidents that led to the divorce. She was able to focus on events that held special memories for her, and through this process she learned that her parents' breakup was much more complex than she could have imagined and had developed over time.

Strategy #5 helped Heather understand that the problems in the marriage were her parents' and not hers, and that she was not the cause of their breakup but the effect of it. She reversed the progression, taking responsibility for her own unhappiness and feelings of guilt, and then visited her desired outcome, which was to find some harmony living with parents in two separate homes. By voicing her needs and talking about the things she wanted to change, she was able to regain control of her life and move forward. The Seven Strategies of Common Sense acted as a road map to her recovery. We can all learn from Heather's example.

## *Making Sense of Strategy #6*

1. Imagine you are going to write your auto-biography. Instead of telling your entire life story, however, your book is going to focus on just one of your major accomplishments, an achievement of which you are especially proud.
2. Begin by creating in your notebook an outline for your autobiography. List the chapter headings in chronological order, and make sure each chapter deals with a major step in your success.
3. After you have a satisfactory outline, begin to increase the detail by listing all the sub-headings you plan to include. Keep increasing the detail in this way until you feel ready to start writing.
4. Using your outline as a guide, complete each chapter with as much detail as possible. Be sure to call on all your sensual memories — not just what you saw, but also what you smelled, tasted, felt, and heard.
5. When you're finished, go back and re-read what you've done. Pay particular attention to the sense-related memories. Note how they added so many more layers of detail to the picture you were trying to paint.

## *Conclusion*

By now, you have realized that you have created a unique path for yourself. Sometimes diversions from that path are enjoyable and even helpful, but if you lose your way entirely, Strategy #6 is there to get you back on track. But one troubling question remains unanswered: What happens if the path you have chosen is the wrong one? This is why you also need our seventh and final strategy.

*Strategy*

**7**

# DON'T BE AFRAID TO CHANGE HORSES IN MIDSTREAM

*The man who makes no mistakes is*
*the man who never does anything.*
— ELEANOR ROOSEVELT

Of the Seven Strategies of Common Sense, this final one could well be the most important. It is designed to help you realize when it is time to cut your losses. Too often, we are caught in a downward spiral that can lead only to disappointment and failure. We *need* to believe that the choices we have made are the correct ones, and so we cling to a losing game plan despite evidence that it is leading us into disaster. This is when we need to implement our final strategy.

Here's a simple example of this phenomenon. Let's say you have just made a long-distance phone call. The call is answered by a recorded message that provides you with a generous list of options. You press the correct buttons and ultimately get a message that says, "You are in priority sequence. Your call is important to us, and the next available operator will help you." So you wait, at the mercy of someone else's choice of background music. Every once in a while, the music stops and the message is repeated, encouraging you to hang on. But you are paying for the call, and in your mind's eye you can see your bill mounting. How long should you wait? When do you decide that enough is enough and hang up? That quick question you were calling about is now costing you more than the answer is worth — more, in fact, than several phone calls would have cost. The solution is to invoke Strategy #7.

## Don't Fight a Losing Battle

One of the hardest lessons to learn in life is that sometimes situations don't work out, despite your best efforts. When you sense things are going this way, you must at some point look at the situation and re-assess the direction you have chosen. There's no logic in wasting energy fighting a losing battle. You have to know when you have reached a point at which it would be wasteful, wrong, or even dangerous to continue. Sometimes this involves facing the unpleasant suspicion that you were wrong to begin with.

For most of us, this is no small feat. Again and

again, we see people flouting logic and reason and betting it all on a long shot. Gamblers make that one last wager just to see if their luck has changed. Criminals try to pull off that one big heist. Abused spouses stay with their tormentors, fully believing that the abuse will never happen again.

For those of us watching from the sidelines, it's easy to see the faulty logic. We know this is not commonsensical. But if you are in the middle of such a situation, it can be difficult to see it clearly. You can be so blinded that common sense fails you. Fortunately, our seventh strategy tells us when it's time to pick up our marbles and go home. You have to know when to cut your losses.

Of course, this strategy is not designed to tell you to give up the minute things go wrong. Instead, it teaches you to recognize when it would be foolish or wasteful to continue. You can see analogies for this in other areas of your life. If you invest in the stock market, for example, a good broker will tell you the importance of setting limits for yourself, of making your goals clear before you begin. Determine the maximum amount you are willing to lose and a target amount you'd like to earn, then instruct your broker to sell once your stock reaches either of these thresholds.

Without clear limits, you run the risk of being trapped in a situation you can't get out of. If your stock starts to rise, it can be very tempting to say to yourself, "It is bound to go up just a bit more." And if it drops, you may want to say, "It has to turn around." Either way, you cling on. By setting limits, you curb temptation and invest in a knowledgeable and deliberate fashion. Now the trick is to transfer this knowledge to all aspects of your life.

### *Here Comes That Inner Voice Again*

If you're having trouble in your relationship, conflict with your kids, or upheaval at work, you don't necessarily pack up and leave. Nor do you ignore the difficulties and hope they will go away by themselves. You need to seize control of the situation and attempt to remedy it. Often this necessitates a return to that inner voice we met in previous chapters.

Up until this point, the voice has been nattering away at us, telling us the truth in all situations. "The inner voice makes [the world's movements] so apparent to me that I cannot watch the course of the sun without imagining a force which drives it," wrote Jean-Jacques Rousseau. The voice is an extremely complex mechanism, and for that reason it demands a more detailed examination. Let's look at the writing process to help us understand how it works.

Many writers create work on paper first without editing it. This frees them to explore new possibilities and ultimately create more powerful and insightful writing. But this type of writing is not ready for publication the moment it's done. First, it must be edited substantively for content, flow, and continuity. Then it must be checked, line by line, for grammar, syntax, and spelling. Once this part of the process is complete, the article or story is ready for submission. But to get to this point, we needed three things: an interesting idea, the words that made this idea a reality, and the detailed examination of the whole work that makes it publishable.

The voice in our head also has three parts to it: the thinker, the doer, and the critic. All three are important, but they must work in harmony to make the seven strategies effective. Strategy #7 will work properly only if all three parts are understood, respected, and ultimately heard.

The *thinker* is the part of the voice that develops new ideas or provides new solutions to the challenges we face. It is the innovative component that creates raw ideas. The thinker focuses exclusively on solutions, without paying any attention to their implementation. For many writers, the thinking component works overtime. In fact, most writers carry a pen and paper around at all times, to record their moments of inspiration. But they have to guard against over-inspiration, against jumping around from project to project without seeing anything through.

The *doer* turns the ideas conjured by the thinker into reality. Many writers keep files of ideas. When they have a quiet spell, they will scour these files, looking for something interesting to write about. The doer then assesses each idea for its feasibility and the amount of research needed to bring it off.

Let me illustrate this with another example. Say you wake up one day and your thinker tells you, "I need a new car!" The doer in you then says, "I could save up and pay cash, borrow the money and pay it off monthly, or see if Aunt Harriet will loan it to me." The doer takes the thinker's ideas and finds ways of making them happen. These two parts must work together before you can accomplish anything.

This brings us to the third part of the voice — the *critic.* The critic balances the thinker and the doer. It watches from the wings with impartial eyes. Like a true critic, it is honest and relentless. You can ignore it or disobey it, but it will not go away. The critic adds its wisdom to the work of the thinker and the doer, refining the decision or even quashing it. When you're thinking about your new car, the critic might say, "I am already overextended, and if I take on more debt I will have to give up something else — maybe a vacation." To the writer, the critic might say, "That idea is dated. You should think of something else." Often what looked like a great idea in the beginning seems not nearly so clever in the cold, hard light of day.

## The Critic on Demand
The thinker, the doer, and the critic have separate voices, each with a distinct message. All are inte-

gral to the success of any endeavour. The thinker and the doer could destroy the whole process if left unchecked by the critic. But what good are ideas (the voice of the thinker) if they remain unexplored? And what good is planning (the voice of the doer) if there is nothing to plan?

These three voices operate in a logical sequence. We need to listen first to the thinker, then to the doer, and finally to the critic to make Strategy #7 work as it was intended. Every voice has its purpose. If each is listened to in equal proportion and in the right sequence, you will be able to avoid no-win situations. But invoking each voice individually can be tricky.

Some actors use a piece of clothing or jewellery to help them prepare for a role. Once they find the right object to put them in the right mood, they use it to help them become the character they are creating. Similarly, a writer might actually change clothes when writing different characters. Clothes, jewellery, moving into a different room — all seem to help us summon different voices.

Can you call up the critic on demand? Yes, certainly. Remember, the critic is always patiently (and sometimes impatiently) waiting in the wings, ready to voice its opinion. The most effective way of calling it up is to dissociate yourself from the problem — turn away from the voices of the thinker and the doer, in other words. Most times, your critic is jumping up and down, waiting to speak. Listen to it!

Unfortunately, we are usually most comfortable in the roles of the thinker and the doer. Often the critic is a pain in the butt, so we ignore it. But ignoring the critic is a recipe for disaster. Among other things, it tells us when to engage Strategy #7 and get out of situations that aren't working.

So how do you dissociate enough from the thinker and the doer to summon the voice of the critic? Well, let's imagine you are chairing a meeting that has been convened to discuss a series of missed deadlines. Everyone in the meeting is scrambling to cover their behinds. They are busy making excuses and blaming others. But all you can see is a waste of time and money. Before you get caught up in the various arguments, put aside the thinker and the doer and become the critic. Sit back in your chair and watch the action. You will find that once you have dissociated yourself from the rest of the team, a new perspective will emerge. You are no longer a defensive or angry participant, but have become an impartial spectator. You will be able to see all the components of the problem and how they have built up, and as a result you should be able to see where the errors lie and suggest ways to minimize your losses.

There are a few ways of reaching your critic. The first, as we've just seen, is to mentally remove yourself from the situation. A very wise person I once met (who is also my role model for someone with common sense) told me that if I could look at life through the fifth-floor window, everything would become clear. This is meant to suggest a position far enough from the situation to afford a view of the whole picture and yet close enough to show the details.

The second method of reaching your critic is to change your physical stance and attitude. Let's go back to our emergency staff meeting. There, you sat back in your chair and watched. You actually changed your posture by assuming the body language and facial expression of the critic rather than that of the thinker or the doer. Instead of hunching over the table in attackmode, ready to pounce on the next person who said the wrong thing, you sat back and observed. Maybe you steepled your fingers thoughtfully, nodded your head wisely, and assumed a detached, relaxed mien. This is the mode of the critic.

It's important to understand that we express each voice differently. To show you what I mean, let me tell you about an employee of a successful politician I know. This employee is a bright man who can always come up with new and exciting solutions to things. He has a great deal of potential, and over the years he has suggested many daring innovations. However, each time his boss dissented, this employee's feelings were hurt. Something had to be done.

One day, the politician noticed how his employee's physical appearance changed whenever he was introducing a new solution to a problem. His eyes opened wide, his posture improved, his hand gestures increased, and his face came alive. So the politician said to him, "Your thinker is working overtime." The employee was completely unable to understand this comment. So the employer continued: "You know that you have two other voices, right? Let's try an experiment. How would your doer respond to this idea?" He explained the role of the doer, and immediately the man's whole attitude changed again. His posture became a little more rigid and his eyes started to narrow. As the doer, the employee then told his boss how his idea would work. The politician repeated the experiment with the voice of the critic and watched again. As always, the employee's idea was viable, but as the critic he was able to move through it quickly and refine it. He turned a merely good idea into a truly great one just by assuming these different roles.

## Actions Have Consequences

So once you have dissociated yourself from events, what should you be looking for? Well, sitting back and observing can be enlightening in and of itself, but your critic also needs to look for the logical consequences of any activity. For every action, there is a logical consequence. If you spend too much money on one thing, you won't have enough for other things. If you drive carelessly, you will increase your chances of having an accident. If you eat badly, you will damage your health. It's a matter of probabilities. While it's always possible to drive carelessly and never have an accident, eat junk food and never feel the effect, smoke until you are a hundred without developing cancer, you are playing against the odds. It is a little like playing blackjack with your life. Do you stand with sixteen or draw? John F. Kennedy was once quoted as saying, "There are risks and costs of action. But they are far less than the long-range risks and costs of comfortable inaction." Let your critic highlight the logical consequences of your actions and help inject some common sense into your decisions.

Now we must accompany the critic back through each of the Seven Strategies of Common Sense. As a critic, you will first look at any situation and realize that nothing is absolute. There is always an alternative answer, and to find that answer you must learn to ask the right questions. That is Strategy #1. Strategy #2 informs you that better solutions are available somewhere. You just have to remove your blinkers and look.

The third strategy explains how to filter and process information, and Strategy #4 demonstrates how to convert information into knowledge by following the three guiding principles: sense of purpose, commitment, and inner strength. Strategy #5 tells you that if a better way is not immediately obvious, you should look in the opposite direction. Reverse the cause-and-effect progression, visit the desired outcome, and clearly state your intentions.

Strategy #6 explains how things can go wrong unexpectedly. It shows you how to retrace your steps and rerun events in ascending order of detail. Finally, Strategy #7 explains when to bail out. This principle teaches you to differentiate between the three aspects of your inner voice: the thinker, the doer, and the critic. The critic looks at actions in terms of their logical consequences.

## *Making Sense of Strategy #7*

1. In your notebook, list five things you would like to do in your life. Assume that there are no restrictions, such as time or money.
2. Next, decide how you could achieve each of these five things. For the purposes of this exercise, do not edit. Try to be truly creative and find ways to accomplish what you want.
3. Now let your critic go to work and re-examine all your notes. Can you then make sense of some of the things you want? Are there feasible ways of accomplishing them?

## *Conclusion*

You may not always be *right* with common sense, but it can always help to make things *better.* If you learn how to balance the thinker, the doer, and the critic, you will be able to meet whatever challenge is in your path and tackle whatever life throws at you.

# A *Final Word*

So these are the Seven Strategies of Common Sense. Now that you understand them, nothing should ever be the same for you again. Your life and your outlook can only be better, more fulfilling, more successful.

But you may be asking yourself if you really have to go through all seven strategies before taking any action. The answer is yes. You do. However, once you have made friends with these strategies, and once they have become part of your thinking, revisiting any one of them becomes automatic. You will not need to proceed mechanically from one strategy to the next because you will have become an unconscious competent.

But it takes time to reach that level. For now, work at the strategies consciously and try to apply them to your life in a methodical fashion. With practice, the strategies will become second nature. You will turn to them instinctively whenever you find yourself groping for a solution or wondering what move to make next. But remember: bringing common sense into your life need not be done at the expense of fun, adventure, and risk. A healthy dose of each is part of a well-balanced life.

That is it. The seven strategies. Now you are ready to bring common sense into your life — and keep it there.

# *Epilogue*

In addition to being the author of this book, I'm also a professional speaker. I travel all over the world, speaking to audiences on a variety of topics. I find this work incredibly rewarding, but what's even more rewarding is when people come up to me after one of my seminars and tell me that something I've said has struck a chord or altered the way they think about things.

That very thing happened after I gave a seminar last fall on the strategies I outline in this book. I had been speaking to a group of bankers, and Dan, a middle manager in the bank's on-line division, approached me after the seminar was over.

"That was so interesting," he began. "I've always just assumed that I knew everything about common sense, but when you break it into categories, it somehow seems so much easier to actually use."

"All of these ideas are things you already knew," I replied. "I think it helps just to have someone to guide you through the process."

"That's exactly right," Dan said. "I feel as though you've given me a road map. I might have got to the same location on my own eventually, but it would have been much easier for me to get lost along the way."

Just then, Mia, a senior executive with the same bank, and Lyle, her executive assistant, walked up and joined us.

"Sorry to interrupt," Mia began, "but I just wanted to thank you for what you said today. It's especially interesting to hear you say that our first instincts are probably the right ones to follow. We're in the middle of restructuring, and I have spent weeks making decisions that are contrary to that strategy. In the end, I'm not really sure that we took the best path. I think it was so hard to decide because I wasn't listening to my intuition at all. Had I done that, the choices might have been easier to make."

"Last week," Lyle piped in, "we were preparing the final report for the board. We had spent a week planning it, compiling the numbers, and drafting the text. When we were close to having the thing completed, the stock market dipped. Suddenly, we were put in a place where we had to rethink everything. It seemed as if all that work had been a giant waste of time. What had made perfect sense a day before now made no sense at all. We had to go back and start from scratch, rethink our plan. These seven strategies will give us a solid base to work from in the future."

Dan jumped in. "I know what you mean, Lyle. With our on-line banking, we found we were making decisions based solely on our experience with the technology; we were forgetting to take into account our corporate mandate to provide sound customer service. We were making decisions that were completely out of balance with the Values and Experience Scale you talked about with the third strategy, Barry. Too much time was being put into the nuts and bolts of how it worked, and not enough thought was going into how a customer would actually use it. Looking back now, I can see we probably spent eight weeks on a project that should have taken us four."

"That's a really important lesson you've just learned," I said. "You should share that with your colleagues. It's crucial in any organization to remember the key values, something that often gets lost in the everyday crunch for the bottom line."

Dan looked puzzled for a moment. "I hear what

you're saying, Barry: hindsight is always 20/20. But how do we know when we're making the right choice in the first place? My biggest problem is that I listen too carefully to my inner critic. I find that I can become paralyzed by doubt, to the point that I can no longer distinguish between the inner voice guiding me and my own sense of self-doubt. Sometimes I get so far away from being the unconscious competent that I end up in a situation where I can't make any decision at all."

"There's no easy solution to that problem," I said, "except to be aware that we learn the most from our mistakes. You can't be afraid of failure. You just have to include the experience of failing in your decision-making process the next time. Our own personal histories are a collection of experiences, some positive and some painful. But all play a critical role in shaping who we are today, and in explaining why we think the way we do. The intelligent person accesses this catalogue of experience and weighs it with his or her values, intellect, and emotions. This increases your odds of making a sound decision the first time."

"But what do we do about issues that really don't make any sense?" Mia asked. "What about things like environmental damage, global warming, pollution, the hole in the ozone layer? It doesn't seem as if we're headed in a direction that makes much sense at all. Yet we charge ahead, clear-cutting forests and polluting the water around us. How can we make sense of something that doesn't really seem to make any sense to begin with?"

"That's an excellent question," I replied. "As a society, we seem to be able to justify all sorts of things: cute little fridge magnets, laptop computers, chip-bag clips, watches, microwave bacon fryers. These things seem to make our lives easier, but once we're done with them they will remain forever in our garbage dumps. We never stop to evaluate whether any of it makes sense, whether we really *need* it. Someday scientists will dig all of this up and judge us as a society. We can only hope that they'll look kindly on us, but who knows? By being conscious and making decisions based on the Seven Strategies of Common Sense, we have some hope of establishing now what scientists of the future will inevitably find out."

Lyle thought for a moment. "It's interesting," he said. "With the tools you've given us — the seven strategies and how to implement them — I feel like we've set off on what promises to be a pretty incredible journey."

"Thank you so much, Barry," Dan said after a long pause. "I've really learned a lot today. I can't wait to share this information with some friends of mine. I'm pretty sure they'll appreciate what you have to teach."

"Thanks," I said to them as they left the room, but I knew I hadn't told them anything they hadn't heard before. I had simply helped them put a framework around what they already knew — and that's just common sense.

### Continuing the Search for Common Sense

We all have grappled with situations that seemed impossible and then found the perfect solution. I would be interested in hearing your own stories of finding common sense in your everyday lives. Perhaps I will be able to use them as inspiration for the people in my workshops, and even as fresh material when it's time to update *Bumblebees Can't Fly.* If you'd like to share your personal experiences with me, log on to:

www.bumblebeescantfly.com

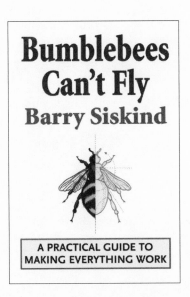

**Bumblebees Can't Fly**

**Barry Siskind**

**A PRACTICAL GUIDE TO MAKING EVERYTHING WORK**

Could someone you know benefit from reading *Bumblebees Can't Fly*? This book makes a great gift for anyone looking for a way to make everything work.

To purchase more copies of this book or to find out more information about how you can have Barry Siskind talk to your company about *Bumblebees Can't Fly*, visit **www.bumblebeescantfly.com**, in North America call toll-free 1-800-358-6079, or write:

International Training and
Management Company
16436 Shaw's Creek Road
Terra Cotta, Ontario
L0P 1N0
CANADA